SCIENTIFIC AMERICAN EDUCATIONAL PUBLISHING

IT'S MENTAL

10 FUN MEMORY AND PSYCHOLOGY EXPERIMENTS

BRING SCIENCE HOME

Published in 2023 by Scientific American Educational Publishing in association with
The Rosen Publishing Group 29 East 21st Street, New York, NY 10010

Contains material from Scientific American , a division of Springer Nature America, Inc., reprinted by permission as well as original material from The Rosen Publishing Group .

First Edition

Editor: Kristen Nelson
Designer: Rachel Rising

Activity on page 5 by Science Buddies, Megan Arnett (March 28, 2019); page 11 by Science Buddies, Megan Arnett (February 28, 2019); page 17 by Science Buddies, Megan Arnett (October 18, 2018); page 25 by Science Buddies, Svenja Lohner (June 7, 2018); page 31 by Science Buddies, Sabine De Brabandere (May 17, 2018); page 35 by Science Buddies, Megan Arnett (September 21, 2017); page 41 by Science Buddies, Ben Finio (October 6, 2016); page 47 by Science Buddies (March 10, 2016); page 52 by Science Buddies (December 11, 2014); page 56 by Science Buddies on December 19, 2013.

Photo Credits: pp. 4, 5, 11, 17, 25, 31, 35, 41, 47, 52, 56 Anna Frajtova/Shutterstock.com; pp. 5, 8, 15, 17, 22, 28, 29, 33, 34, 35, 39, 43, 44, 50, 51, 52, 55, 59 cve iv/Shutterstock.com.

All illustrations by Continuum Content Solutions

Cataloging-in-Publication Data
Names: Scientific American.
Title: It's mental: 10 fun memory and psychology experiments / Scientific American.
Description: New York : Scientific American Educational, 2023. | Series: Bring science home| Includes bibliographic information, glossary and index.
Identifiers: ISBN 9781684169788 (pbk) | ISBN 9781684169795 (library bound) | ISBN 9781684169801 (ebook)
Subjects: LCSH: Experiments-- Juvenile literature | Memory-- Juvenile literature | Science projects-- Juvenile literature
Classification: LCC BF375 S35 2023 | DDC 153 --dc23

Manufactured in the United States of America

CPSIA Compliance Information: Batch #CWRYA23. For further information contact Rosen Publishing, New York, New York at 1-800-237-9932.

CONTENTS

THESE ACTIVITIES INCLUDE SCIENCE FAIR PROJECT IDEAS.

INTRODUCTION

The brain is the body's hub for identifying what the senses take in and collecting memories about our lives. But memory, and even our senses, can be tricky sometimes! In these experiments, you will test short-term memory, examine the role ink color plays in reading, work to detect a lie, and more—all using what scientists know about the brain.

Projects marked with include a section called Science Fair Project ideas. These ideas can help you develop your own original science fair project. Science fair judges tend to reward creative thought and imagination, and it helps if you are really interested in your project. You will also need to follow the scientific method. See page 61 for more information about that.

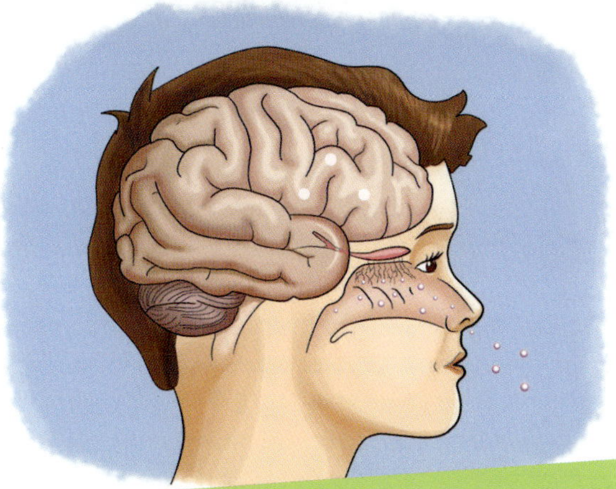

Scentsational Memories

HOW WELL CAN YOU NAME THAT SCENT? FIND OUT WHAT THE NOSE KNOWS—WITH THIS ODIFEROUS ACTIVITY!

Did you know that approximately two million people in the U.S. have no sense of smell? Lack of smell is a disorder known as anosmia and can be caused by damage to the nerves that transmit information from your nose to your brain. Our sense of smell serves an important purpose. We use it to distinguish between edible and inedible items in our lives, including foods that are fresh or rotten. Even particular poisonous chemicals have strong, unpleasant smells. In this activity you will test the scent perception of your volunteers and learn about how smell is associated with memory.

PROJECT TIME

20-30 minutes

KEY CONCEPTS

Biology
Senses
Olfaction
Brain
Memory

BACKGROUND

Your sense of smell is also known as olfaction. Olfaction takes place when molecules known as odorants bind to specific receptors in your nasal cavity inside your nose. When activated, these receptors transmit information along sensory nerves to the olfactory bulb, a neural structure at the base of your brain that transmits smell information from your nose to deeper brain structures. Many of these deeper structures are involved in scent processing as well as in memory and emotion. As a result, our scent memories tend to be strongly linked with memories. Many of the areas that receive scent information are especially old in terms of brain evolution and existed before the areas that give us consciousness. It is often difficult to consciously identify and label a smell. Instead, we often associate scents with the memories and emotions that they evoke.

In this activity you will be testing scent memories in your volunteers and learning about how we remember and recall scents!

MATERIALS

- Ten distinct, concentrated scents. These can be food extracts (such as vanilla) or essential oils (such as peppermint). One possible list of 10 includes: vanilla, almond, cherry, banana, cinnamon, lemon, coconut, orange, chocolate, and mint extracts. Use single scents rather than blends.
- Small zip-top bags (10)
- Cotton balls (10)
- Permanent marker
- Several pieces of paper
- Pen or pencil
- At least one volunteer
- Timer or stopwatch

PREPARATION

- Use your permanent marker to label your zip-top bags with the numbers 1 through 10.

- Place a cotton ball into each bag.
- Assign a number and bag to each extract or essential oil. Make a list of each extract or oil and which number bag it will be in on a piece of paper.
- Pour a small amount of the designated extract into each bag (just enough to dampen the cotton ball). Seal the bags once the extract has been added.
- Create a chart on another piece of paper with 11 columns and three rows. Label the first column "Bag Number," and note the number for each bag here. Label the middle column "Scent, First Guess" and the third column "Scent, Second Guess."
- On a third piece of paper, list—in no particular order—all of the scents you have chosen.

PROCEDURE

- Have your volunteer sit at a table with the bags spread out in front of them. Give them a writing utensil and the chart you created.
- Tell your volunteer that they have three minutes to smell and attempt to identify the scents in each bag. Ask them to write down their best guess next to the bag number in the column "Scent, First Guess" in the chart you provided. *How accurately do you think your volunteer will be able to identify the scents?*
- When your volunteer opens the first bag, start your timer.
- Do not answer any questions that your volunteer asks or help them in any way as they smell each bag.
- After three minutes have gone by, ask your volunteer to stop and close all of the bags.

- Tell your volunteer they will get another two minutes to guess, this time with the aid of the list you created of the scents in random order. Tell them this list has all of the scents included in the activity but not in the same order. This time they will be matching the scent to the bag with the aid of the list.
- Hand them the list facedown. Tell them that when they flip over the list, you will start your timer. This time they should write all of their guesses in the column "Scent, Second Guess."
- Start your timer when they turn over the list.
- At the end of the two minutes ask your volunteer to stop and reseal all of the bags.
- Count the number of correct answers in each column. *Which task was easier for your volunteer?*

SCIENCE FAIR IDEA

Try this activity with another volunteer—but this time split the bags into two groups. Have them guess the first five scents with no reference list, and the second five scents with a list. *Which one was easier for your volunteer?*

SCIENCE FAIR IDEA

Try mixing two smells together and see which are easier and more difficult for your volunteers to identify, mixed smells or single smells.

OBSERVATIONS AND RESULTS

In this activity you probably found that your volunteers had a much easier time identifying the smells when they had a reference list to use. In the first trial, when the volunteer tried to guess the smells without knowing the possible choices, they may have written down less descriptive guesses, such as "candy," "cookies," or "candle." When you gave them a list to use as a reference, however, your volunteer likely had a much easier time correctly identifying the scents in each bag.

Your olfactory system transmits information to brain areas of the limbic system associated with memory and emotion. As a result, we often have difficulty labeling scents by their name—instead we identify them by their associated memories. You might smell the scent of cinnamon and name it as "holidays" because it is common to associate the smell of cinnamon with that time of year.

Because scent memories are associative, and thus somewhat difficult to label correctly, your volunteer probably had fewer correct answers in the first column of their chart. Once you gave them the reference sheet, however, you provided more specific options. It was likely much easier for your volunteer to match the scent with the correct label than it was for them to identify the scents without a reference list.

CLEANUP

Throw out the bags and cotton balls you used. Replace the other materials where you found them.

Tricky Taste Test

Do You Taste with Your Eyes?

WOULD A DRINK BY ANY OTHER COLOR TASTE AS SWEET? LEARN HOW OUR SIGHT IMPACTS HOW WE EXPERIENCE FLAVOR.

Have you ever tried adding green food coloring to your milk? Or blue coloring to the butter you spread on your bread? You might not have tried this, but for years scientists have been studying the effect of color and food appearance on how we perceive food tastes. Believe it or not, our eyes are an important part of tasting and perceiving food! In this activity, you will learn about how you can trick your taste buds—with just a little food coloring!

PROJECT TIME

20-30 minutes

KEY CONCEPTS

Biology
Senses
Perception
Brain

BACKGROUND

The taste buds on your tongue detect flavors and help you identify the foods you eat. Other senses, however, also play a role in how we experience our foods. You probably know the aroma of foods can have a strong effect on how they taste, but did you know the appearance of food also changes how we experience it? Because we usually look at food before putting it in our mouths, the very first information your brain gets about any particular food often comes from the eyes!

From an early age, we learn to associate colors with flavors. When something is orange, we expect an "orange" flavor. If you tasted orange pudding, you would be surprised to find it had a mint flavor. Discrepancies between the appearance of foods and their tastes can make it more difficult to identify the flavoring.

Research has shown the appearance of food can dramatically affect how it tastes to us. In one study, participants ate a plate of normal-looking steak and French fries. All the participants said they enjoyed the food, and it tasted fine. When the lights were brightened, however, it was revealed that the steak was dyed a blue color, and the fries were green. When they saw this, many of the participants refused to eat any more of the food—and a few even became sick.

In this activity, you will be exploring how the appearance of the food we eat affects how it tastes. Don't worry, there won't be any blue meat!

MATERIALS

- At least three volunteers
- Large bottle of apple juice
- Blue, green, and red food coloring
- At least nine clear disposable cups (three for each volunteer)
- Permanent marker
- Piece of paper
- Pen or pencil
- Three regular water glasses
- Water
- Table where you and your volunteers can sit
- Timer or stopwatch

PREPARATION

- Prepare the drinks ahead of time. It's important that your volunteers don't know that there is apple juice in each cup! The idea is that your volunteer should expect something different in each cup. Therefore, don't let them see you preparing the drinks.
- Use your marker to number the clear cups. Label three of the cups with the letter "A," three cups "B," and the remaining ones "C." (That will give you three cups for each volunteer.)
- Add one-quarter cup of apple juice to each clear cup.
- Line up in rows all the cups labeled A; all those labeled B; and all the C cups.
- Add at least two drops of blue food coloring to the A cups. (If necessary, with this and the other colors, add more to darken.)
- Add two drops of green coloring to the B cups.
- Add two drops of red coloring to the C cups.
- *What color do you think will be volunteers' favorite? What about their least favorite? Why?*
- Use your pen and paper to make a chart with five columns (or two more than the number of volunteers that you have) and four rows. Label the first column, "Letter on Cup"; the second column, "Volunteer 1"; the third column, "Volunteer 2," etcetera; and the final column, "Total." Label the second row, "A"; the third row, "B"; and the fourth row, "C."
- Fill the three drinking glasses with water.

PROCEDURE

- Have your first volunteer sit down at the table. Line up one of each of the cups labeled A, B, and C in front of your volunteer. Also give them a glass of water.
- Ask them to start by drinking some water as a palate cleanser.
- Tell your volunteer you want them to taste the drink in cups A, B, and C, drinking water in between each. They have two minutes total to taste the drinks. Once they've tasted the drink in each cup, they should rate them from the one they liked the best to the one they liked the least. Your volunteer can taste each cup more than once, but should drink water in between each taste. Let your volunteer know you cannot provide any information about what is in the cups or respond during the sampling.
- Have your volunteer start the test. As they taste their first cup, start your timer or stopwatch. Remember to not answer any questions or react to anything your volunteer says!
- After two minutes, stop your timer and tell your volunteer to stop tasting.
- Ask which drink was their favorite. In the Volunteer 1 column, mark their favorite cup with the number 3. If your volunteer said the cup B drink was best, for example, you would write number 3 in the B row under Volunteer 1.
- Ask your volunteer which drink they liked least. In the Volunteer 1 column, record their least favorite cup with the number 1.
- Write the number 2 in the remaining row.
- Repeat these steps with your remaining volunteers. Record their responses in the corresponding columns.

- Add the values across each row and record the totals in the Total column. If Volunteer 1 gave a 2 rating to cup A, Volunteer 2 rated cup A a 1, and Volunteer 3 rated cup A a 2, you would record 5 in the Total column for cup A. *Which cup has the highest total? Which has the lowest? Were there any patterns in which cup the volunteers seemed to prefer? Did these match your expectations?*

EXTRA

At the end of the activity have your volunteers close their eyes and taste the juice in each cup again. *Do they notice a difference in how the juice tastes, compared with when their eyes are open?*

OBSERVATIONS AND RESULTS

In this activity, you tested whether the color of a liquid impacted your volunteer's perception of the liquid's taste. Despite the fact each cup contained the same thing (apple juice), you probably found your volunteers preferred the taste of the juice in one of the cups over the others. Because the only difference between the liquids was the color, we can determine from this activity that the appearance of the liquid affects how it tastes.

If any of your volunteers noticed the cups all contained the same thing, compliment them on their acute taste perception! We rely so heavily on visual information, it often influences how we perceive information coming from our other senses. If any of your volunteers were able to separate the visual information from what they were tasting, their perceptions are especially sharp!

CLEANUP

Dump out any remaining water and juice into the sink. Put any remaining apple juice in your refrigerator. Wash the tasting cups to be used again. Put back the other materials where you found them in your home.

Don't Forget!

A Memorization Exploration

LEARN HOW YOU MIGHT BE ABLE TO IMPROVE YOUR MEMORY WITH A BRAIN-TESTING ACTIVITY YOU'RE NOT LIKELY TO FORGET.

PROJECT TIME

40-50 minutes

KEY CONCEPTS

Brain
Cognition
Learning
Memory

What did you have for breakfast last Monday? What color is the floor in your favorite classroom? If you don't remember the answer to these questions, that's okay! Your brain is doing exactly what it is supposed to do. Our brains are nearly perfect storage devices, and part of their perfection is that they know what information to store and what to throw away. Imagine your house if you never tossed anything out—how quickly would it become full of garbage and waste? Your brain is the same way; it stores the information that is useful and important to you and discards the rest. Sometimes your brain remembers things without you consciously telling it to. (You remember the way to your bedroom without ever having had to tell your brain to memorize this information.) Other times we have to tell our brains that information is important. We can do this by paying close attention—and employing a few memory tricks!

BACKGROUND

Learning and memory are the subjects of a tremendous amount of research and study. Although there is still a great deal to learn about these brain processes, we do know two of the most important factors for how well we remember something include how closely we are paying attention and whether the memory relates to something we already know. If you aren't paying attention when someone tells you something, there's a good chance you aren't going to remember what that person said. (This is why your teachers are always telling you to "pay attention!") We also tend to form strong memories in novel (new) situations. For example, you can probably recall the first day of the school year much more clearly than the fourth or fifth. Once we get used to a new situation, our memories tend to be fewer and less specific. Many memory tricks, by contrast, involve taking new information and associating it with something you already know. For instance, if you want to remember that the capital of Mississippi is Jackson, you might imagine your friend Jack swimming in the Mississippi River. Our minds love recognizing patterns and relationships between new and old information. If you can find ways to help your mind do that, you can improve your ability to store and recall information.

In this activity you'll be exploring the memory capacity of a couple volunteers and trying out one technique for improving memory known as chaining.

MATERIALS

- Baking tray
- 24 small household objects (suggestions include: battery, paper clip, rubber band, coin, key, clothespin, key ring, glue stick, toothpick, safety pin, magnet, lip balm, bottle cap, thumbtack, rubber eraser, crayon, pen cap, dental floss, piece of gum or candy, sticker, pebble, small toy, sticky note, tea bag)
- Wax or parchment paper (enough to cover the baking tray several times)
- Black marker
- Several pieces of note paper
- Pen or pencil
- At least two volunteer subjects
- Roll of paper towels
- Stopwatch or timer

PREPARATION

- Do all of your preparation somewhere private, so your volunteers can't see your tray before you start the activity!
- Have volunteers be present separately so the second volunteer does not see the activity while the first volunteer is participating.
- Spread the parchment paper over your baking tray.
- Use your black marker to draw a grid on the parchment paper that is four columns across and three rows down. Use all of the space provided by the paper. Number each cell of your grid 1 through 12 starting with 1 at the upper-left corner, filling the first row left to right before starting the second row with 5 on the left side (12 will be in the bottom-right corner). Make the numbers small and inconspicuous.
- Arrange your household objects so there is one object in each grid cell.
- Carefully cover the tray with a paper towel so your volunteers can't see the objects.

PROCEDURE

- Have your first volunteer sit across from you at a table. (Make sure the second one isn't present for this part of the activity.) Place the covered tray between your volunteer and you.
- Tell the participating volunteer you're going to allow 45 seconds to look at the tray. During that time, they should try to memorize as many of the objects on the tray as possible. When the time is up, you will cover the tray again and ask them to write a list of all the objects they remember. *Do you think it will be easy for them to remember most of the items they see?*
- When your volunteer is ready, uncover the tray and immediately start the timer.

- Remain quiet during the 45 seconds your volunteer is looking at the tray. (Don't allow your volunteer to write anything down during this time.)
- When the 45 seconds are up, cover the tray and place it under the table so your volunteer can no longer see it.
- Give your volunteer a piece of paper and a pen, and ask them to get ready to list all of the objects they remember.
- Start your timer again, and allow your volunteer to spend 1 minute and 30 seconds listing the objects they remember. When the time is up, take the list from your volunteer.
- Uncover the tray and compare your volunteer's list to the objects on the tray. Next to each object on their list, write the number of the grid cell that object occupied. For example, if there was a rubber band in cell 3, write "3" next to "rubber band" on your volunteer's list.
- Underneath your volunteer's list, write down each object they forgot and the corresponding grid cell number. For example, if there was a pebble in cell 8, and your volunteer didn't write pebble on their list, write "pebble, 8."
- Ask your volunteer to turn and face away from you. Remove all of the objects from the tray, and replace them with the 12 objects you didn't use the first time. Cover the tray again.
- Before your volunteer turns around, read this paragraph out loud: "Chaining is a technique that can help improve your ability to remember and recall information. It is a form of visualization that involves picturing the object you're trying to remember. Chaining is especially useful when you have several items you want to remember. To remember the objects, link them together by thinking of images or situations that connect them. For example, if you're trying to remember a grocery list that includes apples, milk, eggs, and bread, try chaining these items together in your mind by imagining apples floating in

milk. Then imagine eggshells filled with milk. Finally picture an egg sandwich with lots of bread. This technique can help you remember by creating associations between the objects you want to memorize. Now you can try it with this activity!" *Do you think your volunteer will remember more objects with this method?*

- Explain that you're going to repeat the activity, allowing them 45 seconds to remember as many objects as possible, and this time they should try this technique when they're memorizing the objects.
- When your volunteer is ready, uncover the tray and immediately start your timer.
- When the 45 seconds is over, cover the tray and place it under the table so your volunteer can no longer see it.
- Give your volunteer a piece of paper and a pen, and ask them to list all of the objects they remember.
- Start your timer again, and allow your volunteer to spend 1 minute and 30 seconds listing their recalled objects. When the time is up, take the list from your volunteer.
- Uncover the tray and compare your volunteer's list with the objects on the tray. Next to each object on their list, write the cell number that object occupied.
- Underneath your volunteer's list, write down each object they forgot and the corresponding grid cell.
- Compare your volunteer's first list and second list. *Which time did your volunteer remember more items?* Notice which cell numbers you listed next to the items they forgot. *Did they always forget the object in a certain cell? Did they always remember the objects in a certain cell?*
- Ask your volunteer if they used the chaining memory technique. And if so, *did it help them memorize the objects? Did they remember more objects during the second time?*

- Repeat the whole activity with your second volunteer. Compare their performance with that of your first. *Did either of your volunteers improve on their second try? Did you notice any patterns related to which objects they remembered or forgot? What about which cells they remembered or forgot?*

SCIENCE FAIR IDEA

Try repeating this activity, but test increasing or decreasing the time allowed for volunteers to memorize the tray. *Does the time make a difference? If so, at what point does it make less of a difference?*

OBSERVATIONS AND RESULTS

In this activity, you tested your volunteer's short-term memory capacity and then tested the effect of chaining, which is one of the many techniques that can help improve someone's memory and recall.

Results for this activity will vary slightly across different people—every mind is different! You might, however, have noticed some consistent patterns. For example, you may have found both of your volunteers remembered the first or last objects (the ones in squares 1 and/or 12) more clearly than the objects in the middle of the tray (for example, in squares 6 and 7). If this is the case, this could have to do with two memory characteristics known as recency and novelty.

In the case of recency, we tend to remember things more clearly when they just happened. If someone tells you a number and asks you to repeat it back to them, it's much easier to repeat it right after they tell you compared with repeating it the next day. In this case, your volunteer might have viewed the last objects on the tray (the ones in squares 11 and 12) right before the time ran out. These objects might, therefore, be easier to recall.

The earliest objects (in squares 1 and 2), by contrast, might have been the first ones your volunteer noticed. In this case, the activity was still new and novel to your volunteer. Our brains love novelty—you'll notice that in their day-to-day lives most people don't sit and stare straight ahead; their eyes are continuously moving around, taking in new information. Our minds are often sharpened by new situations, and in those cases we tend to have clearer memories of the things we noticed first. If your volunteers remembered the early objects (in squares 1 and 2) the best, it might be because they were especially interested in the task when they first saw those squares!

In the second part of this task, you explored whether the memory technique known as chaining had any effect on your volunteers' ability to recall the objects. This technique is very effective for some people, in part because our brains are good at making associative memories. We often (unconsciously) look for patterns or relationships to help us remember things. For example, when you meet someone named Tom you might immediately think of someone you already know with the same name. This helps you remember the new Tom's name. In the case of chaining, you are creating associations between the objects—even when they don't exist. If your volunteers found it helpful, suggest to them they should try it in everyday life!

CLEANUP

Put the 24 items used in the experiment back where you found them. Throw out the used parchment or wax paper, or keep them to reuse in a craft.

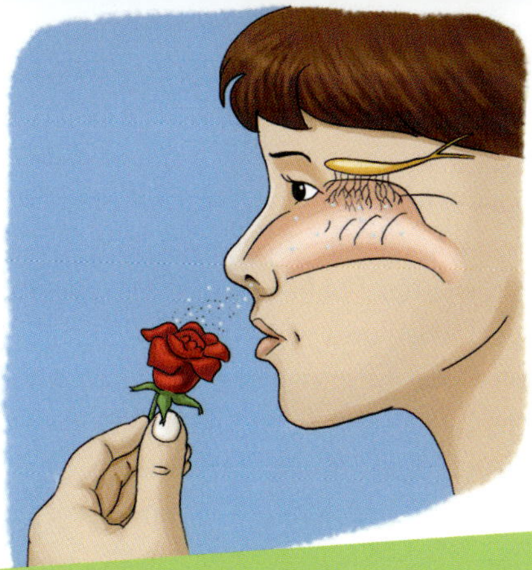

Play a Memory Game with Your Nose!

WHAT CAN YOU TELL BY SMELL? TEST YOUR SMELL SENSITIVITY WITH THIS MEMORY CHALLENGE!

Whether it is freshly baked cookies, smoke from a wood fire or a bouquet of roses—your nose is an amazing smell detector! Your sense of smell cannot only identify a huge variety of odors, but it is also incredibly sensitive. Think about how easily you can detect if someone in your neighborhood is having a barbecue just by smelling hints of smoke from a faraway grill. But how good is your nose when it comes to differentiating individual smells? Try this activity to find out!

PROJECT TIME

20–30 minutes

KEY CONCEPTS

Brain
Perception
Senses
Smell

BACKGROUND

Every day you are surrounded by a vast variety of odors that your nose is able to pick up. Your sense of smell, also called olfaction, is very powerful. Everything that has an odor releases specific chemicals, called odorants, into the air. These odorants eventually reach your nose, and when you inhale, they get transported deep into the space behind your nose. There you have millions of smell receptors able to detect specific odorants. You can imagine this process like a lock-and-key mechanism where each odor molecule fits into one specific receptor inside your nose. Once the receptor binds to the chemical, it communicates with the brain by sending a signal, and your brain is able to identify the specific odor.

But what makes one scent different from another? Thousands of chemicals exist that trigger the sensation of smell, and each individual one—and combinations between them—will result in a different smell and signal pattern in your brain. Researchers now believe we can distinguish up to one trillion (an amount more than 100 times the world's human population) different scents, meaning individual odorants as well as mixtures! Sometimes only a single chemical distinguishes a specific smell—and many people, especially in the food industry, try to produce them to make artificial scents. One example is a chemical molecule called vanillin that, as you might guess, smells like vanilla.

It is not only the individual molecule that matters—its concentration is also important. You are much more likely to smell a specific odor if there are many of the odor molecules around. If there are only a few, you probably will not even notice them. Put your nose to the test in this fun game of flavor memory!

MATERIALS

- Four different flavor extracts, such as vanilla, mint, almond, and cinnamon extracts
- Four 8-ounce (236 ml) plastic cups or glasses
- 16 mini 2-ounce (59 ml) plastic cups with lids
- Water
- Spoon
- Medicine dropper
- Measuring cup
- Tablespoon
- Masking tape
- Permanent marker
- Several volunteers (optional)

PREPARATION

- Label eight mini cups so you have two for each flavor. Write the labels on the bottoms of the cups so you cannot see them from the top.
- Add 1 tablespoon (15 ml) of each extract to the respective mini cups.
- Put a lid on each cup and set them all aside. This is your first set of smell samples.
- For the second set, label each of the four 8-ounce cups with one of your chosen flavors.
- Fill each 8-ounce (236 ml) cup with 1/2 cup (118 ml) of room temperature water.
- Using the medicine dropper, add one drop of your first flavor to the respective cup and mix with a spoon.
- Repeat this step for the other flavors. Make sure to rinse the medicine dropper and spoon in between each flavor.
- Again, label eight mini cups so you have two mini cups for each flavor. Write the labels on the bottoms of the cups so you can't see them from the top. Add a "2" after each flavor to mark them as your second set of smell samples.
- Add 1 tablespoon (15 ml) of each of the flavored solutions into the respective labeled mini cups.
- Put a lid on each cup and set them aside. This is your second set of smell samples.

PROCEDURE

- Take your first set of smell samples and shuffle them so you do not know which cup contains which flavor.

- Now the game begins. Pick up one cup, bring it close to your nose, open the lid and smell inside. Close your eyes, or make sure not to see the label of the cup while you smell the sample. *What flavor do you pick up? Can you easily identify it?*

- Next, you have to find the second cup with the same flavor. Pick up each cup and smell its contents until you find the one cup that you think contains the same flavor. Put the matching flavor pair aside without looking at the labels. *Was it difficult or easy to find the matching flavor?*

- Now, move on to the next flavor and try to find the matching cup again. Repeat this with all the remaining cups, until you have found all the four matching flavors.

- Check the labels to see if your guess was right. *Did you get all of your flavor pairs right?*

- Put all the cups of the first sample set aside and get all the mini cups of the second sample set.

- Again, shuffle the cups, so you do not know which ones belong together. Spread the cups out in front of you and repeat the steps of the matching test with your second sample set. Make sure you do not see the label of the cups while you smell the samples. *Was it easier or more difficult to identify the flavors this time? Why do you think this was the case? Were you able to identify all the matching flavor pairs?*

EXTRA

If you have volunteers, repeat the whole activity with more people. *How well can they identify the flavors in the first sample set compared with the second set?*

EXTRA

Add more flavors to the game. *What about banana extract or orange? Does it make the game easier or more difficult?*

EXTRA

What if you added a third sample set, where you add one drop of each flavor to 4 cups (946 ml) of water. *Can you still identify and match all of the flavors?* If yes, try to make even more dilutions (for example, adding one drop to 10 cups [2.6 l] of water, etcetera) and test if your nose is still able to pick up the odorants in these samples.

OBSERVATIONS AND RESULTS

You probably thought this game was very easy with the first sample set. The flavors in the extracts are very concentrated. This means that in each of the solutions there are a lot of flavor molecules. When you smell these cups, lots of molecules move up into your nose and reach its smell receptors. Once the molecules bind to the receptors, your brain is able to identify the specific smell. It should not have been a problem for you to find the matching flavor pairs because each of the flavors has its unique flavor molecule that generates a very specific signal pattern in your brain. This allows us to differentiate among scents.

In the second sample set, it was probably more difficult to find the matching flavor pairs. This is because you diluted your flavor extract by adding one drop to 1/2 cup (118 ml) of water, which means there were fewer odor molecules in each of your samples than before. There needs to be a certain amount of odorant in the air—the odor threshold concentration—before smell receptors can send enough signals to the brain to identify a specific odorant. This threshold can differ between people as well as flavors because of their different chemical properties. If you still smelled all your samples correctly in the second sample set, try to find your odor threshold for each of the flavors by diluting the samples even more!

CLEANUP

Dispose of your flavor solutions in the sink. Wash the cups to be used again. Put the other materials you used back where you found them.

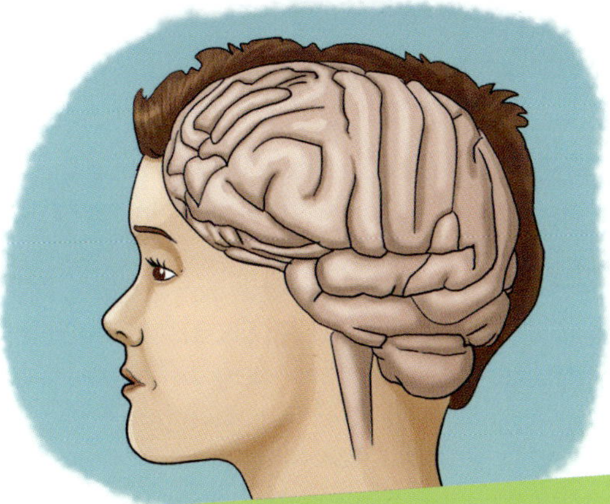

Memory Surprises

TEST YOUR MEMORY WITH THESE SURPRISING TRICKS—YOU MIGHT BE SURPRISED BY HOW EASY IT IS TO FOOL YOUR BRAIN!

Have you ever wondered why some things are easy to recall whereas others need hours of study? For example, you might be able to recollect what happened at your birthday party without any practice, but you need hours of study before you can recite a few lines for a theater play. Our mind stores and remembers information in fascinating ways. Remember to do this activity, and you will be surprised at what your memory can do for you!

PROJECT TIME

15–30 minutes

KEY CONCEPTS

Brain
Psychology
Memory
Cognition

BACKGROUND

You might have noticed human memory often fails to produce an exact replica of what was, but it excels at creating a reconstruction or interpretation. If you hear a story or explanation, you quickly pick up the essence of it. Your mind jumps in to classify, label, fill in, or even distort details so the story or explanation makes sense to you; it makes connections to knowledge already in your memory. That interpretation can be stored in your memory and is rather easy to recall—much easier than remembering an exact copy of the story or explanation you heard. It takes a lot of effort to store an exact copy so that you can reproduce it later.

There might be a reason why nature has evolved in such a way. This flexible method of storing information allows you to more easily combine separate ideas and make connections—or to recognize the known in unknown situations. You can change your viewpoint and change how you remember things accordingly. It seems memory is designed so we can easily use and generalize our recollections, which lets us plan and do better in the future—a valuable survival skill! Being able to remember exactly what happened or what was said, read, or heard might not be as important for survival.

MATERIALS

- Paper
- Pencil
- Partner (if you would like someone to read a written list for you)
- Volunteers (optional)

PREPARATION

- Gather your materials, and get ready to test your memory.

PROCEDURE

- Read the following list of words, or ask your partner to read the list aloud for you: bed, dreams, cozy, rest, night, tent, blanket, yawn, snore, nap. We will come back to this list later in the activity.

- Draw a familiar object from memory. If you use money, draw a coin or bill you use frequently. If you are not that familiar with money, choose an object you use or see frequently that has a fair amount of detail. It could be the wrapper of your favorite snack, a soap bottle, a piece of artwork hanging in your living room, etcetera. It is important to add as many details as you can remember. Do not worry about your drawing skills—this activity is about remembering details. *Is it easy to recall how the object looks? Do you feel unsure about some of the details?*

- If you have the object you drew available, compare your drawing with the real object. *Are the details in your drawing placed correctly? Did you accurately remember how the object looked? If you did, why do you think this was the case? If you did not, why do you think it can be hard to accurately remember how objects look—even the ones you see frequently?*

- Back to the list of words—here are three: bed, car, and sleep. *Which of these words was or were part of the original list? How sure do you feel about your answer?*

- Look back at the list or have someone read the words for you. *Were you correct?*

- If you are like most people, you thought "sleep" was part of the list, but it was not. *Why do you think most people think this word was part of the original list? What could this tell us about memory?*

EXTRA

Do you think it is necessary to distract the mind between hearing or reading the list of words and the question about which words were part of it? Find some volunteers to try it out!

EXTRA

Do you think the list: paper, story, reading, magazine, school, study, pencil, and chapter can trick people into believing the word "book" was part of it? Why do you think this? Be sure to test it on some volunteers!

EXTRA

Can you create a list of words that can trick people into believing a different word was part of it?

OBSERVATIONS AND RESULTS

Was it hard to accurately remember the details of an object you see frequently? Were you convinced "sleep" was a word that appeared in the list? If that was the case, you are like most people. Your memory rarely records an exact copy of what was. Rather, it reconstructs what was while keeping what our mind identified as the essence intact.

Your memory stores enough information to easily recognize objects you see or use frequently because that is all you need to perform well in daily tasks. Unless you paid very close attention to the details at some point in the past, your memory did not store them, therefore you cannot recall them when asked to make a drawing. If you compared your drawing with the real object and identified the details that were distorted or left out, you will probably remember more details the next time you draw this object. Paying attention in a meaningful way helps build memory.

The test with the 10 words also shows how your memory is good at recalling the general idea—the concept—but not the exact words. Did you notice all the words in the list revolve around the concept of sleep? The mind picks this up and remembers it—and when asked later, it is convinced "sleep" was part of the list.

CLEANUP

Put away your materials where you found them.

Don't Forget!

Test and Trick Your Short-Term Memory

CAN YOU TRICK YOUR SHORT-TERM MEMORY INTO WORKING BETTER? GATHER SOME VOLUNTEERS AND FIND OUT!

If someone tells you to remember a phone number or address, it can feel like an easy task at first. You repeat the numbers to yourself, either aloud or in your mind. But after just a few seconds you might find yourself starting to doubt your own memory. Was it 5-7-3 or 3-7-5? Our brain is always seeking new and useful information, and as a result, it will try to throw away information that seems old or irrelevant, such as a random string of numbers or an address. There are ways of helping our minds retain information, however, and in this activity, you will explore ways that we lose and keep memories.

PROJECT TIME

20–30 minutes

KEY CONCEPTS

Psychology
Learning
Memory
Brain

BACKGROUND

Short-term, or working, memory is a way of describing most people's abilities to store a small amount of information for a brief period of time in a readily accessible form. Short-term memory has a short duration (thought to be in the order of seconds or minutes) but is quickly and easily accessed. People don't have to stop and think to remember something in short term memory—they can access it quickly and easily.

There are many techniques for improving memory retention (capacity to store information over time). Such techniques include visualizing the information in a surprising way or linking pieces of information together so that one reminds you of the other. In the case of visualizing information, this could be as simple as remembering you parked your car on the fifth floor in the D section by picturing five dogs sitting in your car! In addition, linking information could help you remember your grocery list. If you need to purchase cereal, milk, fruit, cheese, and eggs, you could imagine the cereal in a bowl, with milk pouring over it and pieces of fruit on top. Then imagine cracking an egg over everything, and it's full of melted cheese! These may seem simple or even silly, but they are time- and scientist-tested for improving memory retention. In this activity, you'll test the recall of a few friends or family members and learn a few tricks for improving memory!

MATERIALS

- Piece of paper
- Pen or pencil
- At least four volunteers
- Quiet place to test your volunteers
- Clock or timer

PREPARATION

- Use your pen and paper to create a table with five columns and five rows. Label the columns' top boxes accordingly:
    - first column: "Volunteer Name"
    - second: "Single Digit 1 Minute"
    - third: "Single Digit 2 Minute"
    - fourth: "Multiple Digit 1 Minute"
    - fifth: "Multiple Digit 2 Minute"

PROCEDURE

- Test each of your volunteers individually, following the steps below. Make sure they don't hear each other's tests!
- Start with Volunteer 1. Take them into the quiet space you've chosen for testing.
- Write Volunteer 1's name in the second row of your table, in the column "Volunteer Name."
- Tell Volunteer 1 that you're going to be asking them to memorize four different sets of numbers. You will tell them the number sequence once, then wait a designated amount of time before testing how well they remember the number sequence.
- When your volunteer is ready, read the 1 Minute Single Digit Number Sequence aloud to your volunteer: "4, 9, 1, 7, 2, 2, 6, 5, 8, 3." As soon as you finish reading the sequence, start your timer. *How many numbers do you think your volunteer will be able to correctly remember in the right order?*
- Make sure to stay quiet so you don't distract your volunteer. After one minute has gone by on your timer, ask your volunteer to repeat the sequence back to you. As they recite the numbers aloud, write down the numbers as they say them in the "Single Digit 1 Minute" column.
- Tell your volunteer you're going to read another set of numbers, and ask them to memorize and repeat them after a certain amount of time.
- Read the next Single Digit Number Sequence aloud to your volunteer: "5, 0, 2, 8, 8, 3, 7, 6, 9, 4." As soon as you finish reading the sequence, start your timer. *Do you think your volunteer will be able to remember the same amount of numbers as in the one-minute test? Why or why not?*
- After two minutes have gone by, ask your volunteer to repeat the sequence back to you. As they say the numbers aloud, write them down as they repeat them in the "Single Digit 2 Minute" column.

- Tell your volunteer you're going to read a third set of numbers, and ask them to memorize and repeat them after a certain amount of time.

- When your volunteer is ready, read the Multiple Digit 1 Minute Sequence aloud to your volunteer: "49, 17, 22, 65, 83." As soon as you finish reading the sequence, start your timer. *Do think your volunteer will have a more difficult or an easier time remembering these 10 digits?*

- After one minute has gone by, ask your volunteer to repeat the sequence back to you. As they say the numbers aloud, write them down as they recite them in the "Multiple Digit 1 Minute" column.

- Tell your volunteer you're going to read a final set of numbers, and ask them to memorize and repeat them after a certain amount of time.

- When your volunteer is ready, read the Multiple Digit 2 Minute Sequence aloud to your volunteer: "50, 28, 83, 76, 94." As soon as you finish reading the sequence, start your timer. *How do you think your volunteer will do trying to remember these numbers in order?*

- After two minutes have gone by, ask your volunteer to repeat the sequence back to you. As they call out the numbers aloud, write them down as they say them in the "Multiple Digit 2 Minute" column.

- Circle the mistakes your volunteer made in each column.

- Repeat these steps with your remaining volunteers. (Make sure your next volunteers can't see the numbers from previous volunteers on the paper.)

- Add up the number of mistakes made in each column. *Which column has the highest number of mistakes made? Which column has the lowest? Why do think that might be?*

SCIENCE FAIR IDEA

Try repeating the test, but instead of remaining quiet while your timer is going, ask the volunteer to sing a common song. Test what effect this has on their ability to repeat the number sequence.

OBSERVATIONS AND RESULTS

You might have noticed the digits you read for the Single Digit and Multiple Digit number sequences were the same. For the Single Digit Number Sequence, however, you read 10 individual numbers whereas for the Multiple Digit Number Sequence you read five double-digit numbers. Although they contain the same number sequence each time, you might have noticed your volunteers found it easier to memorize the Multiple Digit Number Sequence. Your volunteers were able to remember the number "49" as one number whereas when you said it as "4, 9" they had to remember the numbers 4 and 9 as distinct numbers. To remember information such as number sequences, your brain uses its short-term memory storage. Your short-term memory has a limited amount of space to store information. As you fill it, there is less room to hold additional content. The number "49" takes up less space in your memory than the numbers "4" and "9" do separately. This is a memory technique known as "chunking," and it can help you memorize longer sequences of numbers (and letters) by chunking them together.

You might have also noticed that more errors were made when the volunteer had to wait longer to repeat the number sequence back to you. Attention and time are extremely important to short-term memory function. As more time goes by, it's more difficult to control our attention. Even when we try to focus on a piece of information such as a number sequence, retaining that information over longer periods of time becomes more difficult. This is sometimes referred to as the recency effect, where the more recently something was discussed, the easier it is to remember.

CLEANUP

Put away your materials.

A B C D E F
X Y Z A B C

Crack the Code!

Make a Caesar Cipher

CAN YOU SEND SECRET MESSAGES TO A FRIEND IN PLAIN SIGHT? TRY A CAESAR CIPHER AND SEE!

If you need to send a secret message to a friend, how could you prevent other people from reading it? One way is to encrypt the message—that is, use a secret code that only you and your friend know. Try this activity to learn how to create your own "Caesar cipher," a popular type of code that is easy to learn.

PROJECT TIME

30 minutes

KEY CONCEPTS

Patterns
Code
Puzzles
Cryptography

BACKGROUND

Cryptography is the study of writing or solving secret codes that are used for secure communication. Historically, codes have been used by politicians, spies, and countries at war to prevent their enemies from knowing what they're up to. Many of the earliest codes, or "ciphers," such as the one you will create in this project were easy to create by hand. Now cryptography is essential in computer science for keeping everything from e-mails to bank account information secure.

The Caesar cipher, named after Roman Emperor Julius Caesar, is one of the earliest and most widely known ciphers. It is a simple form of a "substitution cipher" where you replace each letter of the alphabet with another letter by shifting the whole alphabet a certain number of letters (wrapping around to the beginning once you reach the end). For example, this would be your key and code if you shift each letter by three spaces:

Plain: A B C D E F G H I J K L M N O P Q R S T U V W X Y Z
Cipher: X Y Z A B C D E F G H I J K L M N O P Q R S T U V W

So, when you write your message, the letter A gets replaced with X, B gets replaced with Y, and so on. For example, the word "HELLO" reads:

Plain: H E L L O
Cipher: E B I I L

In order to decode your message, you need to share the "key" (the number 3) with your friend. After that, you can send messages that are written in cipher so other people can't read them!

MATERIALS

- Pencil and paper
- At least one other person

PREPARATION

- Explain the concept of a Caesar cipher to a friend or have them read the Background section of this activity.
- Write down the alphabet from A to Z.

- Pick a number from 1 to 25. (If you use 26, you will just wind up with the original alphabet.) This number is your key.

PROCEDURE

- Shift the entire alphabet by the number you picked and write it down below your original alphabet (as shown on p. 42).
- Pick a message to write to your friend. It might be easiest to start out with a simple message (such as a single word or phrase) before you try longer sentences or paragraphs.
- Write down your encoded message using your shifted alphabet. If it helps, write down your plain text message first, then encode it one letter at a time (such as the "hello" example on p. 42). Just make sure the piece of paper you give your friend only has the encoded message!
- Give your friend the encoded message and tell them the key. *Why do you think you wouldn't want to write down the key?*
- See if your friend can decrypt your message. If it helps for the first try, let them work backward using the original and shifted alphabets you wrote down. Using the example from the Background, the letter X becomes A; Y becomes B; and so on.
- Try switching and using a different key for the same messages. *Do either look easier to crack?*

EXTRA

Try finding a third person who does not know what a Caesar cipher is. *Can they crack your code if they "intercept" your message?*

EXTRA

What if the person who intercepts your message knows about Caesar ciphers? Does that make it easier to crack the code? Because there are only 25 possible keys, Caesar ciphers are very vulnerable to a "brute force" attack, where the decoder simply tries each possible combination of letters. This might take some patience if a human does it, but nowadays computers can unravel the code in a fraction of a second, so Caesar ciphers are not considered a secure method to encrypt electronic communications.

EXTRA

Another way to crack the Caesar cipher is "frequency analysis," which is based on the fact that in natural English speech and writing, certain letters appear much more frequently than others. For example, the letter E appears more often than any other one whereas Z appears the least often. (If you have ever played the board game Scrabble, you might notice that this determines how many points letters are worth!) So, for example, if you read an entire paragraph and notice that the letter D appears more often than any other, odds are that it used a Caesar cipher with a shift of 1 (making E a D in the code). This technique will be more accurate for longer blocks of text and very inaccurate for short words or phrases because there are plenty of words that do not contain E at all. *Can you have a friend write an entire paragraph with a Caesar cipher and then try to crack it using frequency analysis?*

EXTRA

If you plan to use the Caesar cipher for regular communication, one risk is that eventually someone will discover your key. You can help prevent this by changing the key, for example using a new one every week. This is a similar concept to periodically changing your computer passwords.

EXTRA

The Caesar cipher is just one type of substitution cipher. Look up some other types of substitution ciphers and try them out. *Are they harder or easier to use and crack?*

OBSERVATIONS AND RESULTS

Once you and your friend both understand how to use a Caesar cipher it should be relatively easy to send encrypted communications to each other. This can be a fun way to pass secret messages back and forth between friends. As discussed on p. 44, however, although the Caesar cipher provides a great introduction to cryptography, in the computer age it is no longer a secure way to send encrypted communications electronically.

CLEANUP

Put away your materials.

Pinocchio's Arm
A Lie Detector Test

SOMETIMES IT MIGHT SEEM DIFFICULT TO TELL A LIE FROM THE TRUTH. BUT BY LEARNING A LITTLE BIT ABOUT HOW THE BRAIN WORKS, YOU MIGHT BE ABLE TO TELL WHEN SOMEONE IS LYING—WITHOUT FANCY EQUIPMENT! FIND A VOLUNTEER AND SEE IF YOU CAN DETECT A LIE!

You have probably been told that one ought not lie. And you probably hope that people tell the truth to you. But have you ever thought of lying as an interesting social ability? Lying is actually tied to empathy, the ability to see things from another person's perspective. Most humans begin to develop these skills around the age of three, when they begin to understand that what they know about the world might be different from what other people know about the world. Telling lies might be a skill, but lies can, of course, cause trouble. Sometimes you would probably really like to know how to tell a truth from a lie. Will the lie detector proposed in this science project really work?

PROJECT TIME

15-30 minutes

KEY CONCEPTS

Psychology
Brain
Theory of the Mind
Brain states

BACKGROUND

Lying is a process that activates specific parts of the brain. Lying is also often accompanied by a feeling of guilt, which creates stress. Standard lie-detection techniques look for the body's reactions to this stress, such as elevated heart rate or blood pressure, faster breathing, or sweating. This is difficult. How can you distinguish between stress that is related to a lie and other stress, such as the anxiety about taking a lie detector test? Or what if the person telling a lie does not feel guilty about the lie or has learned to stop the body's response to feeling guilty?

Neuroscience provides an alternative method to separate a truth from a lie that uses functional magnetic resonance imaging (or fMRI) of the brain. An fMRI scan shows which parts of the brain receive the most blood—or are the most active—as the brain performs a specific task. These scans reveal that more and different parts of the brain are active during lying, as compared to truth-telling. In short, the brain works harder when it is telling a lie than when it is telling the truth.

Excluding unconscious tasks such as walking and talking, we generally sacrifice efficiency when we do two or more activities at the same time. Do you think it is harder to perform well at a physical task while our brain is busy telling a lie, compared to while our brain is busy telling the truth? Find a friend and see if you can detect a hard-working brain!

MATERIALS

- Volunteer(s)
- Paper and pen or pencil
- If your volunteer(s) are much taller than you, you will need a stable stool or chair on which to stand. If the difference is relatively small, the first or second step of a stair will help. The goal is to have your shoulders at the same level as the shoulders of the volunteer.

PREPARATION

- Inform your volunteer that you would like to test a particular lie detector and need to collect a little information from the volunteer to do so.

- Ask your volunteer to complete the following sentences three times, filling in something different each time. "I strongly dislike ..." Write down the answers or draw a picture of it so you remember what it was.
- Repeat the previous step with the following sentence: "I really like ..."

PROCEDURE

- Have the volunteer stand facing you, a few feet away. If you are much shorter than your volunteer, raise yourself up on a stair, stool, or chair so your shoulders are approximately level with the shoulders of your volunteer.
- Have your volunteer extend their arm straight out in front, palm facing down so the whole arm is at shoulder level. Tell the volunteer you are going to have them say a few phrases, that you will push the arm down, and you would like them to try to keep the arm up.
- Extend your arm straight out and place your hand, palm down, over the volunteer's hand and wrist.
- Ask the volunteer to say the following sentence three times in a row: "I really like ..." where you fill in the blank with the first item your volunteer mentioned in the list they really like, so that this is a truth for your volunteer to say out loud. As the volunteer says the sentences, press down on the volunteer's arm and apply a steady, constant pressure. You do not need to press it all the way down; you just want to get an idea of how hard you need to push to get the arm to move down. *Is it easy or hard to get the arm down?*
- Repeat the previous two steps, replacing the sentence with "I really like to vomit." This phrase is a lie for the volunteer because nausea is universally an unpleasant experience. *Is it easier, similar, or harder to press the arm down compared to*

when the person was telling the truth (previous step)? In other words, was it easier or harder for your volunteer to perform the task of holding up his or her arm?

- Repeat the previous steps, filling in the stated likes or dislikes of your volunteer and rate each time how much resistance you feel, or how difficult it is to get the arm to lower. *Can you see a pattern? Is it easier, similar, or harder to get the arm down when your volunteer is telling a truth compared to when your volunteer is telling a lie?*

EXTRA

Can you also detect specific body language revealing a lie? Pay attention to facial expressions, the pitch of the voice, hand movements, and breathing rate. *Do any of these change when the volunteer tells a lie compared to when the volunteer tells the truth? Why would this be so?*

EXTRA

Test several volunteers. *Does the lie detector work better on some volunteers than others?*

EXTRA

If you feel the lie detector works, test if it passes the "blind" test. In this case, do not tell the volunteer you are testing a lie detector. Instead, only ask the volunteer to perform the task of holding his or her arm up while you push on it and ask the volunteer to tell a few truths and lies that they are okay later revealing whether or not they were truths. *Were you able to distinguish the truths from the lies?*

EXTRA

How is this lie detector test setup different from real-life experiences where you try to uncover a mystery? If you feel the lie detector works in the test setup, do you think it would also work in real-life cases? Why or why not?

EXTRA

In this test, you used a raised arm as the task for the volunteer to do. *Can you find other tasks that better display when someone is telling a lie compared to telling the truth?*

OBSERVATIONS AND RESULTS

You probably felt that it was easier for you to push the arm down when the volunteer was telling a lie compared to when the volunteer was telling the truth. This is what is expected; the volunteer will likely have a harder time fulfilling a physical task while telling a lie.

Neuroscientists have discovered that the brain works harder when it is telling a lie than when it is telling a truth. They found that just four parts are active during truth-telling, whereas seven parts are active during lying. This difference in brain states makes it harder for volunteers to perform a small physical task while telling a lie. As a result, your volunteers had a harder time performing well on the task of holding their arm up while their brains were busy telling a lie, compared to when their brains were engaged in telling the truth.

Telling a lie is often accompanied by other clues, were you able to spot any?

The test situation in this activity is very different from a real-life situation. In this test, the subject is asked to tell a lie and no consequences are attached. In real life, lies are self-generated and more might be at stake. These and other factors might influence how well the lie detector works.

CLEANUP

Put away the materials used.

Seeing Science

Exploring Color Perception with the Stroop Effect

WILL YOUR VOLUNTEERS BE ABLE TO SEPARATE THE COLOR OF INK A WORD IS WRITTEN IN AND THE WORD? TRY THIS EXPERIMENT TO FIND OUT!

Have you ever tried to pat your head with one hand while you rub your stomach with the other? This science activity is kind of like doing that, but it can actually give you some insight into how your brain works. The challenge of this activity is to name colors. It sounds simple enough, right? If you think it does, you should see what happens when words of colors get in the way! This is a fun activity to try out with family and/or friends while spending time together.

PROJECT TIME

20–30 minutes

KEY CONCEPTS

Psychology
Reading
Colors
Perception
Reaction time

BACKGROUND

This activity is an attempt to unravel the workings of thought processes that involve attention, perception, reading, and naming. How does it work? It is an investigation into a phenomenon known as the Stroop effect, which was first described in 1935 in a now-famous experimental psychology paper by John Ridley Stroop. The Stroop effect uses words printed in different colors of ink (such as red, green, or blue) and shows how when those printed words are also the words of colors, it can affect how quickly a person is able to name the color of the ink. For example, if the word "red" is printed in yellow ink it will take a different amount of time for a person to name the color of the ink than if the word "red" is printed in red ink. What is the difference exactly in the time that it takes to say the ink color? Try this activity with some friends and/or family to find out!

MATERIALS

- 10 index cards that are each 3 inches by 5 inches (7.6 cm by 12.7 cm). Alternatively, you could use fewer or more cards that are larger or smaller in size, respectively.
- Scissors
- Ruler (optional)
- Colored markers of five different colors (The colors should be distinctly different, such as green, brown, blue, red, and yellow.)
- Timer or stopwatch
- At least three volunteers

PREPARATION

- Hold an index card vertically and then cut across it twice to make three smaller cards, each about 3 inches by 1.6 inches (7.6 cm by 4 cm). Do this to all 10 index cards so you have created a total of 30 smaller cards.

- On 15 of the small cards, use a colored marker to write the name of the marker's color on the card. For example, you could use a green marker to write the word "green" on one of the cards. Use all five different color markers, and use each marker on three cards. (This means that if you have a green marker, three cards should have the word "green" written on them using the green marker, and if you have a brown marker, three cards would have the word "brown" written on them using the brown marker, and so on.)

- On the remaining 15 small cards, use the same set of colored markers, but this time write a color name that is not the same as the marker's color. For example, you could use the green marker to write the word "blue" on one of the cards. Again, use all five different color markers, and use each marker on three cards.
- Keep the two sets of cards separated.

PROCEDURE

- Get your first volunteer ready and explain what they are supposed to do in this test. Tell them that they will be given a set of cards where each card contains a word written in colored ink and that the task is to call out the ink color of each word as quickly as possible without making a mistake.
- When you are both ready, give one of the sets of small cards to the volunteer and time how long it takes the volunteer to name the colors in the card set. *How long did it take the volunteer to get through the set?*
- Next, give the volunteer the other set of small cards and again time how long it takes the volunteer to name the colors in this card set. *How long did it take the volunteer to get through the other set?*
- Repeat this process with your other volunteers. For each one, switch which set you start them with.
- *Overall, which set did volunteers take the longest amount of time to get through: the set where the words on the cards match the colors they're written in or the set where the words and ink color don't match? Why do you think this is?*

SCIENCE FAIR IDEA

You could try this activity again, but this time use cards with words written on them in matching ink compared with cards that have color words written on them all in black ink. *Do you find a difference in how easily people can read the color words based on whether they're written in matching ink or only black ink?*

SCIENCE FAIR IDEA

Repeat this activity but this time have people look at the cards so that the words are upside down. *Is there still a Stroop effect when the cards are used this way?*

OBSERVATIONS AND RESULTS

Did you find that people could more quickly go through the set of cards with the words written in matching ink compared with words that were written in a different color ink?

The Stroop effect shows that when a color word is printed in the same color as the word, people can name the ink color more quickly compared with when a color word is printed with an ink color that is different from the word. (For example, when blue ink is used to write the word "blue," the ink color is named more quickly than when blue ink is used to write the word "green.") This is what you should have also seen when doing this activity. For example, you may have seen that it took volunteers around 13 to 17 seconds to get through the matching set of cards but around 20 to 25 seconds to get through the nonmatching set.

One explanation for the Stroop effect is called interference. From the earliest years of school, reading is a task that people practice every day. We become so good at it that we read words automatically. When we are asked to name the color of the word instead of reading the word, somehow the automatic reading of the word interferes with naming the color of the word. This interference effect provides scientists with a measurable means to investigate how the brain works.

CLEANUP

Put away the materials used. Recycle your color cards, or keep them to use another way.

Study Skills Science

Investigating Memory Mnemonics

HAVE YOU EVER FORGOTTEN AN ITEM IN A LIST? THERE'S A WAY TO BETTER REMEMBER LISTS OF WORDS OR ITEMS. FIND OUT HOW EFFECTIVE MNEMONICS ARE IN THIS MEMORABLE EXPERIMENT!

Have you ever needed to remember a long list of words, such as state capitals or items on a shopping list? Even if a list can be full of interesting facts, it can still be hard to remember. But there are some memory techniques that can help a person to better recall a list. In this science activity you'll try out a technique called mnemonics—a memory boosting strategy. You'll investigate whether using mnemonics can help you and your friends or family members remember lists of words.

PROJECT TIME

60–75 minutes

KEY CONCEPTS

Memory
Learning
Brain
Psychology

BACKGROUND

Sometimes it can be difficult to remember long lists of words, which is where memory techniques can help. Any memory trick that can help somebody remember information is called a mnemonic. Mnemonics can use systems of rhymes, acronyms, diagrams, or other techniques to aid a person in recollecting names, dates, facts, figures, and more. An example of a mnemonic is the rhyme, "i before e except after c, or when sounding 'a' as in 'neighbor' or 'weigh.'" This mnemonic was designed to help a person remember the order of the letters "i" and "e" in different words. As was mentioned, mnemonics can also use acronyms, which are words where each letter of the word stands for something. For example, a mnemonic for remembering the names of the Great Lakes uses the acronym HOMES, where each letter stands for one of the lakes: Huron, Ontario, Michigan, Erie, and Superior. People also use mnemonics by mentally turning a list of words into a memorable sentence or a mental image that incorporates all of the words.

MATERIALS

- At least six volunteers, in addition to the person who will be running the activity
- Quiet room for testing
- At least eight scraps or sheets of paper
- Pencil
- Stopwatch or timer

PREPARATION

- Develop a list of words that is at least seven words long. Your list is only limited by your own imagination—you can come up with one by taking inspiration from the world around you, such as making the list correspond to a grocery list or thinking of a group of objects or items.

- Make a corresponding mnemonic for the list of words. When trying to come up with a mnemonic, you can look at the examples given in the Background section. For example, you could come up with an acronym that uses the first letter of each word on the list. Alternatively, if you make a list of words that are descriptive, you could think of a funny sentence or image that incorporates all of those words. *How well do you think your mnemonic will work?*

- On one sheet of paper, write the list of words, but do not include the mnemonic. On a second sheet of paper, write the list of words and include the mnemonic (if it is something that can be easily written down).

PROCEDURE

- In a quiet room, hand one of the sheets of paper (with the list of words) to a group of at least three volunteers. Hand the other sheet of paper (with the list of words and its mnemonic) to a different group of at least three volunteers. To the group that received the list along with the mnemonic, tell or show them how the mnemonic works. (If you are concerned that the other group might hear/see the mnemonic, put the groups in two different rooms or test them at different times.) Make sure that the group that didn't receive the mnemonic does not try to make up one to help them memorize the list.
- Give both groups 5 minutes to study the lists. *How confident do both groups seem about knowing the words at the end of the five minutes?*
- After 5 minutes have elapsed, take away the lists and have the groups do something else for 45 minutes. They can watch TV, talk, listen to music, or perform some other activity.
- After 45 minutes have elapsed, test each member of each group separately. Have each person go back into the quiet room and either recite the words they read on their list or write them on a blank piece of paper. If you want, you can time how long it takes each person to recall the words. *How many words can each person recollect correctly? How long does it take each person to recall their list?*

- ***Does it seem like the people who were given a mnemonic could more quickly remember more of the words on their lists with greater accuracy? Overall, does it look like the mnemonic helped people remember their lists of words?***

EXTRA

Try increasing the wait time from 45 minutes to 1 hour, 5 hours, 1 day and/or longer. *How long does the mnemonic help a person remember their word list?*

EXTRA

There are many different types of techniques that people use as mnemonics to memorize something. For some examples, see the Background section. Try this activity again, but this time use a different type of mnemonic, such as an acronym, a funny sentence that uses all of the words on a list, and/or words that rhyme. *Do some types of mnemonics seem to be more effective for memorizing a list of words than others?*

EXTRA

Instead of testing two random groups of volunteers, try testing four groups of volunteers—two who are relatively young and two who are relatively old (with half of the younger people and half of the older people each receiving the plain lists and the other halves getting the lists with the mnemonic device). *Does using the mnemonic technique help older people recall their lists better than it does for younger people?*

OBSERVATIONS AND RESULTS

Did the people who were given a mnemonic (along with their lists of words) more effectively recall the words than the people who weren't given a mnemonic?

Overall, in this activity you should have seen that people who were given a mnemonic generally recalled their lists of words better than the people who weren't given one. Specifically, the people who received a mnemonic should have remembered more of the words on their lists, and with greater accuracy (making fewer mistakes in recalling what the exact words were) than people who didn't receive a mnemonic (and didn't make up one on their own). The people with mnemonics should have also recalled their entire lists of words more quickly. With the small sample size of volunteers used in this activity, however, the results may not have been as pronounced as they would be in a much larger study. Additionally, some mnemonic techniques can be more effective than others (and certain types work better for some people than others), so that could also affect the outcome of this activity.

CLEANUP

Put away your materials. Recycle the sheets of paper used for the word lists.

THE SCIENTIFIC METHOD

The scientific method helps scientists—and students—gather facts to prove whether an idea is true. Using this method, scientists come up with ideas and then test those ideas by observing facts and drawing conclusions. You can use the scientific method to develop and test your own ideas!

Question: What do you want to learn? What problem needs to be solved? Be as specific as possible.
Research: Learn more about your topic and refine your question.
Hypothesis: Form an educated guess about what you think will answer your question. This allows you to make a prediction you can test.
Experiment: Create a test to learn if your hypothesis is correct. Limit the number of variables, or elements of the experiment that could change.
Analysis: Record your observations about the progress and results of your experiment. Then analyze your data to understand what it means.
Conclusion: Review all your data. Did the results of the experiment match the prediction? If so, your hypothesis was correct. If not, your hypothesis may need to be changed.

GLOSSARY

associate: To think of one thing when you think of another thing.

capacity: The potential for holding or storing.

conscious: Noticing with some controlled thought or observation.

detect: To discover the existence of.

differentiate: To recognize a difference.

dilution: The state of being diluted, or thinned out.

distort: To change to give a false picture of something.

distract: To draw attention away.

extract: Matter drawn out of something by using a machine or chemicals.

identify: To figure out the identity of.

inconspicuous: Not very noticeable.

interpretation: The act of telling the meaning of.

molecule: The smallest part of a substance that has all the properties of that substance.

olfactory: Having to do with the sense of smell.

perception: The result of observing.

perspective: One's mental view of something.

receptor: A cell or group of cells that takes in sense information.

replica: A copy.

technique: The way in which something is learned or understood.

threshold: The point at which an effect occurs.

ADDITIONAL RESOURCES

Books

Feldman, Robert S. *Understanding Psychology*. New York, NY: McGraw-Hill Education, 2021.

Guarino, Robert. *Me and My Memory: Why We Forget Some Things and Remember Others.* San Jose, CA: Hoopoe Books, 2022.

Guarino, Robert. *What We See and Don't See.* San Jose, CA: Hoopoe Books, 2022.

Websites

Discovery Education
sciencefaircentral.com

Exploratorium
www.exploratorium.edu/search/science%20fair%20projects

Science Buddies
www.sciencebuddies.org/science-fair-projects/project-ideas/list

Science Fun
www.sciencefun.org/?s=science+fair

Videos

How Memories Form
ny.pbslearningmedia.org/resource/nvmh-sci-memsform/wgbh-nova-memory-hackers-how-memories-form/

The Nature of Memory
ny.pbslearningmedia.org/resource/nature-of-memory-braincraft/nature-of-memory-braincraft/

Publisher's note to educators and parents: Our editors have carefully reviewed these websites to ensure that they are suitable for students. Many websites change frequently, however, and we cannot guarantee that a site's future contents will continue to meet our high standards of quality and educational value. Be advised that students should be closely supervised whenever they access the internet.

INDEX